OUR HOLIDAYS

STEWART ROSS

Wayland

STARTING HISTORY

Food We Ate
How We Travelled
Our Family
Our Holidays
Our Schools
Shopping
What We Wore
Where We Lived

Series Editor: Kathryn Smith
Series Designer: Derek Lee

First published in 1992 by
Wayland (Publishers) Ltd
61 Western Road, Hove
East Sussex BN3 1JD

© Copyright 1992 Wayland (Publishers) Ltd

British Library Cataloguing in Publication Data
   Ross, Stewart
   Our Holidays (Starting History)
   I. Title II. Series
   790.09

ISBN 0 7502 0250 5

Typeset by Dorchester Typesetting Group Ltd
Printed and bound in Belgium by Casterman S.A.

ACKNOWLEDGEMENTS
Chapel Studios 7 (top), 15 (top), 21 (top), 29 (top); Eye Ubiquitous 16; Sally and Richard Greenhill 26; Hulton *cover*, 7 (bottom), 11, 13, 20, 27; Imperial War Museum 10; Mary Evans 5, 6; Topham 9, 12, 14, 15 (bottom), 17, 19, 21 (bottom), 30 (bottom); Wayland Picture Library 22, 28; Zefa 4, 8, 18.

Words that appear in **bold** are explained in the glossary on page 31.

Starting History is designed to be used as source material for Key Stage One of the National History Curriculum. The main text and photographs reflect the requirements of AT1 (Understanding history in its context) and AT3 (Acquiring and evaluating historical information). The personal accounts are intended to introduce different points of view (AT2 – Understanding points of view and interpretations), and suggestions for activities and further research (AT3 – Development of ability to acquire evidence from historical sources) can be found on page 30.

CONTENTS

What is happening in this picture? The family are going on holiday. Can you see the young girl carrying her suitcase?

Nowadays many people go away for their holidays. Some people travel to warm **foreign** countries. Have you had a holiday away from home?

Do you think this is a modern drawing? Look at the clothes everyone is wearing. The picture shows a crowd of **holiday-makers** over 400 years ago!

At that time a holiday was a special or **holy** day. This is where the word holiday comes from. People did not go away, but they still enjoyed themselves. What are they doing in this picture?

This picture of Margate beach was taken in 1957, over thirty-five years ago. Do you know anyone who was alive then?

Look how crowded the beach is. In those days holidays **abroad** cost a lot of money. Most families went to the seaside in this country for their holidays, or stayed at home.

In 1952, when he was twelve, John Cooper had his first seaside holiday in Brighton.

'We were all very excited because we had never seen the sea before. I couldn't believe how huge it was. It rained all week, but we didn't mind. We went on the pier instead. Dad took this photo of me. I am trying on a silly hat.
Can you see mum's new summer hat? On the last day of the holiday it blew into the sea. We laughed, but she was cross.'

7

What do you think these tickets are for? They are airline tickets for people who are flying abroad on holiday.

Nowadays people buy holidays from a **travel agent**. We can choose where we want to go by looking in a **travel brochure**. The travel agent arranges the holiday for us.

Here are some British people on holiday in Spain in 1974. Were your mum and dad alive then?

In the 1970s many people started to take their holidays abroad. Lots of new **airports** and hotels were built. Why do you think people wanted to take their holidays abroad?

Look at this photograph of a beach. It was taken at the time of the **Second World War**. How can you tell that the picture was taken in wartime?

Few people went on holiday during the War. Some beaches, like the one in this picture, were closed. No one was allowed to sit on the beach or swim in the sea.

These women are on a cycling holiday in 1931. How are their clothes and bicycles different from modern ones?

Cycling holidays were very popular in the 1930s. Many people still enjoy riding their bicycles in the fresh air today. But cycling was much safer sixty years ago. There were not as many cars on the roads.

ALL ABOARD!

Can you guess what these people are doing? They are waiting for a train to take them on holiday. The picture was taken about sixty years ago. Your grandparents might have been alive then.

In those days there were very few cars. Most people went to the seaside by train. Have you been on holiday by train?

Here is a picture from 1935. Do you think it looks like a hotel? It shows the inside of a **liner**!

Before the Second World War most people who travelled abroad went by ship. The journey often took several weeks and sometimes passengers were seasick. But liners were very comfortable and there were lots of things to do on board.

This busy photograph was taken at London Airport in 1961. The passengers are waiting to go on holiday to Spain.

Thirty years ago flying became much cheaper than before. More people could take their summer holidays abroad. The crowds in the airports got bigger and bigger.

Liz Coppin will never forget her first holiday abroad. She went to Majorca.

'It was the first time I had flown in a plane and I was frightened. Majorca was very different from Blackpool, where we had taken our holidays before. It was hot and sunny. My husband got sunburnt and I had an upset tummy. But we got some lovely **souvenirs**. The little jug I bought is still on the shelf at home.'

15

This is a very unusual holiday **resort**. Can you see the hotel? It is by the River Nile, in Egypt.

These days people travel to all sorts of different places. Some people like to visit foreign countries and their cities. Others enjoy exploring different types of countryside, such as mountains or deserts. What sort of holiday do you like best?

This picture was taken in India seventy years ago. Holiday-makers are riding on the elephants' backs. They are going hunting for wild animals.

We do not have this sort of holiday nowadays. Many animals, like tigers, are **protected**. Do you think it is right to hunt wild animals?

SOMEWHERE TO STAY

This block of flats was built just for holiday-makers. It is still very new. There are two large swimming pools at the front. Can you see anyone swimming?

People on holiday stay in all sorts of places. We can stay in hotels, flats or on campsites. Where do you stay when you go on holiday?

This family is camping in a field. They are making camp-beds out of straw. The picture was taken in 1936. Modern tents are often much bigger than those in the picture. Some have windows, real beds and a small cooker. Today campers stay on campsites. These have shops, swimming pools and plenty of games to play.

These people are staying in a boarding house. Many families stayed at places like this when they visited the seaside. Boarding houses are different from hotels. They are ordinary houses where people can stay for the night. You can have breakfast and dinner there too. Many people still like to stay in boarding houses.

In 1946 Jane Bird worked for the summer in a **holiday camp**.

'I can still remember when this photo was taken. That's me, standing on the right, waving to the girls going by.
We didn't go abroad for our holidays, like many people do today. But we still had a wonderful time. I worked at the camp just after the War. Everyone wanted to enjoy themselves. We had bicycle races like this one along the seafront.'

People have always enjoyed sunbathing on the beach and swimming in the sea. But today we know that we must use suntan lotion to protect our skin from sunburn.

People started taking holidays by the sea over 200 years ago! In those days the beaches and the sea were clean. Today some beaches are **polluted**. This is because many people leave rubbish on the beach and in the sea.

Do you know what these people are looking at? They are watching a Punch and Judy show on the beach. The picture was taken over seventy years ago. Do you know anyone who was alive then?

In those days there was no television. Beach shows were very popular with the grown-ups as well as the children. Have you ever seen a Punch and Judy show?

Do you think these holiday-makers are having a good time? Look closely at their faces. The picture was taken on the Palace Pier in Brighton in 1936.

Most large seaside towns had a pier then. They had all sorts of games and amusements on them. Today many piers have fallen down. Have you seen a pier?

This very old photograph was taken in 1919. Your grandparents' mum and dad might have been alive then.

The children are paddling in the sea. Look at their clothes. How are they different from what you wear on holiday?

These children are enjoying an activity holiday. They are learning how to canoe.

Activity holidays are a new idea. You learn how to do different things, meet lots of people and visit new places. There are activity holidays for children and for grown-ups too. Do you know anyone who has been on one?

These girls are on a winter holiday. They are skiing in the mountains where there is lots of snow. How can you tell that this is not a modern photograph?

In the past only rich people went skiing. Today skiing holidays are quite popular. People can **hire** the special clothes and skis they need.

27

These girls come from Japan. They are visiting the USA for the first time and enjoying American food.

Every year **tourists** go on holidays all over the world. It is an exciting way to learn about people from different countries. Where would you most like to go on holiday?

In 1991 Tracy Smith went to the USSR with her mum.

'We had a great holiday. The USSR seemed so far away – I never thought I would go there. But nowadays tourists can fly there quite quickly.

We really liked the people we met. But we couldn't understand what they said.

Here's my mum in the snow, trying to learn some Soviet words. By the end of our stay all she could say was hello and goodbye.'

FINDING OUT MORE

Talking to people

Ask grown-ups you know well if they went on holiday when they were young. They can tell you how holidays today are different from those when they were children. You could get them to speak into a tape recorder. Ask them questions; Where did you go? What was it like? How did you get there?

Using your eyes

Ask a grown-up you know well if they have some photographs you can look at. The pictures on old postcards can show you what seaside towns used to look like. If you live near the sea, have a look in the library for some old pictures of your town. Old books, newspapers, magazines and films can also help you find out how people used to spend their holidays.

Holiday displays

Why not make a scrapbook or display about holidays? Draw a picture of how you like to spend your holidays. Then draw a picture of how someone might have spent their holiday twenty years ago, then forty years ago and so on. Ask if there are any old postcards or photographs at home, which you can use for your work. You might even have some souvenirs from your own holidays to display.

GLOSSARY

Abroad Somewhere outside your own country, like France or the USA.

Airports The places where aeroplanes take off and land.

Foreign Belonging to another country.

Hire To pay for the use of something for a certain amount of time.

Holiday camp A special place where people can go for their holidays. Everything is arranged for them.

Holiday-makers People on holiday.

Holy Religious.

Liner A large passenger ship.

Polluted Made dirty with rubbish.

Protected Kept safe from harm by a law.

Resort A town where people go for their holidays.

Second World War The War which lasted from 1939 to 1945. The fighting spread around the world.

Souvenirs Presents which people bring back from holiday, to remind them of where they have been.

Tourists People who travel around for pleasure.

Travel agent A person who sells holidays.

Travel brochure A magazine which tells you about lots of different holidays. There are pictures of the hotels and beaches.

INDEX